Splash OF Color

4 KNIT DISHCLOTH SETS

I'm a fan of "get knit quick" projects like these cool (or is that hot?) kitchen sets. In no time at all, I could whip up a great dish, cleverly accented by the perfect potholder, dishtowel or dishcloth. Or even better…I could skip the whole cooking thing altogether and order in. I'll have more time to knit! Pick your favorite pattern, grab your needles, and go. When you just can't knit anymore, dial up your neighborhood place and have a favorite dish delivered. You can tell your family it's all my fault, but be sure to send me a photo of the finished project at KnitCrochetEditor@leisurearts.com.

Cheryl

Cheryl Johnson
Knit & Crochet Publication Director

LEISURE ARTS, INC.
Little Rock, AR

TILED DISH TOWEL

◖■◻▱ **EASY**

Finished Size: 11" x 12" (28 cm x 30.5 cm) not including shaped top or hanging loop

MATERIALS

100% Cotton Medium Weight Yarn **MEDIUM 4**
  [1¹/₂ ounces, 68 yards
  (42 grams, 62 meters) per ball]: 2 balls
Straight knitting needles, size 8 (5 mm) **or** size
  needed for gauge
Crochet hook, size H (5 mm)

GAUGE: In pattern,
        18 sts = 4" (10 cm)

DISH TOWEL

Cast on 50 sts.

Note: When instructed to slip a stitch, always slip as if to **purl** with yarn forward.

Rows 1-4: K1 tbl *(Fig. 10, page 28)*, knit across to last st, slip 1.

Rows 5 and 6: K1 tbl, K4, P4, (K2, P4) across to last 5 sts, K4, slip 1.

Row 7 (Right side)**:** K1 tbl, K2, P2, (K4, P2) across to last 3 sts, K2, slip 1.

Row 8: K1 tbl, K4, P4, (K2, P4) across to last 5 sts, K4, slip 1.

Row 9: K1 tbl, K2, P2, (K4, P2) across to last 3 sts, K2, slip 1.

Row 10: K1 tbl, K4, P4, (K2, P4) across to last 5 sts, K4, slip 1.

Rows 11 and 12: K1 tbl, K2, P2, (K4, P2) across to last 3 sts, K2, slip 1.

Rows 13-82: Repeat Rows 5-12, 8 times; then repeat Rows 5-10 once **more**.

Row 83: K1 tbl, K2, P2, [SSK *(Figs. 6a-c, page 27)* K2 tog *(Fig. 5, page 26)*, P2] across to last 3 sts, K2, slip 1: 36 sts.

Row 84: K1 tbl, (K2, P2) across to last 3 sts, K2, slip 1.

Row 85: K1 tbl, K4, P2, (K2, P2) across to last 5 sts, K4, slip 1.

Row 86: K1 tbl, knit across to last st, slip 1.

Row 87 (Decrease row)**:** K1 tbl, SSK, knit across to last 3 sts, K2 tog, slip 1: 34 sts.

Rows 88 and 89: Repeat Rows 86 and 87: 32 sts.

Row 90: SSK 8 times, K2 tog 8 times: 16 sts.

Rows 91-106: K1 tbl, knit across to last st, slip 1.

Rows 107-111: K1 tbl, SSK, knit across to last 3 sts, K2 tog, slip 1: 6 sts.

Bind off all sts in **knit**, place last st on crochet hook.

Refer to Basic Crochet Stitches, page 28.

Loop: Ch 20; being careful **not** to twist ch, slip st in first bound off st; finish off.

DANDY DISHCLOTH

◖■◻◻ **EASY**

Finished Size: 8³/₄" (22 cm) square

MATERIALS
100% Cotton Medium Weight Yarn **4** MEDIUM
  [1³/₄ ounces, 80 yards
  (50 grams, 73 meters) per ball**]**: 1 ball
Straight knitting needles, size 7 (4.5 mm) **or** size
  needed for gauge

GAUGE: In Garter Stitch,
  18 sts = 4" (10 cm)

DISHCLOTH
Cast on 41 sts.

  Note: When instructed to slip a stitch, always slip as if to **purl** with yarn forward.

Rows 1-4: K1 tbl *(Fig. 10, page 28)*, knit across to last st, slip 1.

Rows 5 and 6: K1 tbl, K3, P1, (K1, P1) across to last 4 sts, K3, slip 1.

Rows 7 and 8: K1 tbl, K2, P1, (K1, P1) across to last 3 sts, K2, slip 1.

Rows 9-12: Repeat Rows 5-8.

Rows 13-16: K1 tbl, knit across to last st, slip 1.

Rows 17-64: Repeat Rows 5-16, 4 times.

Bind off all sts in **knit**.

PERFECT POT HOLDER

 INTERMEDIATE

Finished Size: 8" x 7¹/₂" (20.5 cm x 19 cm)

MATERIALS

100% Cotton Mediun Weight Yarn
  [1¹/₂ ounces, 68 yards
  (42 grams, 62 meters) per ball]: 2 balls
Straight knitting needles, size 8 (5 mm) **or** size
  needed for gauge

GAUGE: In pattern,
  18 sts = 4" (10 cm)

POT HOLDER

Cast on 37 sts.

Note: When instructed to slip a stitch, always slip as if to **purl** with yarn forward.

Rows 1-4: K1 tbl *(Fig. 10, page 28)*, knit across to last st, slip 1.

Row 5: K1 tbl, K2, knit increase *(Figs. 2a & b, page 26)* in each stitch across to last 3 sts, K2, slip 1: 68 sts.

Rows 6-14: K1 tbl, K3, slip 1, (K1, slip 1) across to last 3 sts, K2, slip 1.

Row 15: K1 tbl, K2, SSK *(Figs. 6a-c, page 27)* across to last 3 sts, K2, slip 1: 37 sts.

Rows 16-18: K1 tbl, knit across to last st, slip 1.

Rows 19-74: Repeat Rows 5-18, 4 times.

Bind off all sts in **knit**.

COLOR BLOCKS I DISHCLOTH

■■■□ INTERMEDIATE

Finished Size: 8¼" (21 cm) square

MATERIALS
100% Cotton Medium Weight Yarn
[2½ ounces, 122 yards
(70 grams, 111.5 meters) per ball]:
Yellow **and** Orange - 1 ball **each**
[2 ounces, 98 yards
(56 grams, 89.5 meters) per ball]:
Variegated - 1 ball
Straight knitting needles, size 8 (5 mm) **or** size
needed for gauge
Crochet hook, size H (5 mm)

GAUGE: In Garter Stitch,
18 sts = 4" (10 cm)

Note: When instructed to slip a stitch, always slip as if to **purl** with yarn forward.

DISHCLOTH
With Yellow, cast on 15 sts.

BLOCKS 1-3
Row 1 (Right side): Knit across to last st, slip 1.

Rows 2-8: Knit across.

Cut Yellow.

Rows 9-16: With Orange, knit across.

Cut Orange.

Rows 17-32: With Variegated, knit across.

Bind off all sts in **knit**, leaving last st on needle.

BLOCK 4
With **right** side facing and working in end of rows on Blocks 3, 2 and 1, pick up 16 sts *(Fig. 8b, page 27)*: 17 sts.

Rows 1-17: Knit across.

Bind off all sts in **knit**, leaving last st on needle.

BLOCK 5
With **right** side facing and working in end of rows on Block 4 and across cast on edge on Block 1, pick up 24 sts *(Fig. 8a, page 27)*: 25 sts.

Rows 1-23: Knit across.

Bind off all sts in **knit**, leaving last st on needle.

BLOCK 6
With **right** side facing and working in end of rows on Blocks 5, 1, 2, and 3, pick up 28 sts: 29 sts.

Rows 1-7: Knit across.

Bind off all sts in **knit**.

BLOCK 7
With **right** side facing and Yellow, working in end of rows on Blocks 6 and 4 and along bind off edge on Block 3, pick up 29 sts.

Instructions continued on page 6.

Rows 1-5: Knit across.

Bind off all sts in **knit**, leaving last st on the needle.

BLOCK 8
With **right** side facing and working in end of rows on Blocks 7 and 5 and Back Loops Only of bound off edge on Block 4 *(Fig. 9a, page 27)*, pick up 32 sts: 33 sts.

Rows 1-5: Knit across.

Bind off all sts in **knit**, changing to Orange in last st.

BLOCK 9
With **right** side facing, working in end of rows on Blocks 8 and 6 and Back Loops Only of bound off edge on Block 5, pick up 32 sts: 33 sts.

Rows 1-5: K1 tbl *(Fig. 10, page 28)*, knit across to last st, slip 1.

Bind off all sts in **knit**, leaving last st on the needle.

BLOCK 10
With **right** side facing and working in end of rows on Blocks 9 and 7 and Back Loops Only of bound off edge on Block 6, pick up 36 sts: 37 sts.

Rows 1-5: K1 tbl, knit across to last st, slip 1.

Refer to Basic Crochet Stitches, page 28.

Bind off all sts in **knit**, place last st onto crochet hook, slip st across end of rows on Block 10; join with slip st to first bound off st on Block 7, finish off.

Color Blocks I Dishcloth

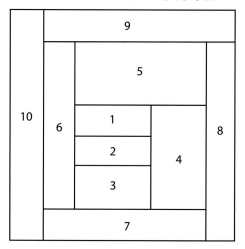

COLOR BLOCKS II DISHCLOTH

■■■□ INTERMEDIATE

Finished Size: 8¹/₄" (21 cm) square

MATERIALS
100% Cotton Medium Weight Yarn
   [2¹/₂ ounces, 122 yards
   (70 grams, 111.5 meters) per ball]:
      Yellow, Orange, **and** Green - 1 ball **each**
   [2 ounces, 98 yards
   (56 grams, 89.5 meters) per ball]:
      Variegated - 1 ball
Straight knitting needles, size 8 (5 mm) **or** size needed for gauge
Crochet hook, size H (5 mm)

GAUGE: In Garter Stitch,
      18 sts = 4" (10 cm)

Note: When instructed to slip a stitch, always slip as if to **purl** with yarn forward.

DISHCLOTH
With Yellow, cast on 2 sts.

BLOCK 1
Row 1 (Right side)**:** Knit increase *(Figs. 2a & b, page 26)*, slip 1: 3 sts.

Row 2: K1 tbl *(Fig. 10, page 28)*, knit increase, slip 1: 4 sts.

Rows 3-20: K1 tbl, knit increase, knit across to last st, slip 1: 22 sts.

Cut Yellow.

BLOCK 2
Row 1: With Green, K1 tbl, knit across to last 3 sts, K2 tog *(Fig. 5, page 26)*, slip 1: 21 sts.

Rows 2-18: K1 tbl, knit across to last 3 sts, K2 tog, slip 1: 4 sts.

Row 19: K1 tbl, K2 tog, slip 1: 3 sts.

Row 20: K1 tbl, K2 tog: 2 sts.

Bind off all sts in **knit**.

BLOCK 3
With **right** side facing, Variegated, and working in Back Loops Only of slipped sts at end of rows *(Fig. 9b, page 27)*, begin at Row 20 on Block 1 and pick up 16 sts along edge of Block 1: 16 sts.

Rows 1-11: Knit across.

Bind off all sts in **knit**, leaving last st on needle.

BLOCK 4
Working in Back Loops Only of slipped sts at end of rows on Blocks 3 and 1, pick up 22 sts: 23 sts.

Rows 1-11: Knit across.

Bind off all sts in **knit**, leaving last st on needle.

BLOCK 5
Working in end of rows on Block 4 *(Fig. 8b, page 27)* and in Back Loops Only of slipped sts at end of rows on Block 2, pick up 22 sts: 23 sts.

Rows 1-11: Knit across.

Bind off all sts in **knit**, leaving last st on needle.

BLOCK 6
Working in end of rows on Blocks 5 and 3 and in Back Loops Only of slipped sts at end of rows on Block 2, pick up 28 sts: 29 sts.

Rows 1-11: Knit across.

Bind off all sts in **knit**.

BLOCK 7
With **right** side facing and Green, working in end of rows on Blocks 6 and 4 and in Back Loops Only of bound off edge on Block 3 *(Fig. 9a, page 27)*, pick up 28 sts: 29 sts.

Rows 1-5: Knit across.

Bind off all sts in **knit**, leaving last st on needle.

BLOCK 8
Working in end of rows on Blocks 7 and 5 and Back Loops Only on bound off edge on Block 4, pick up 32 sts: 33 sts.

Rows 1-5: K1 tbl, knit across to last st, slip 1.

Bind off all sts in **knit**.

BLOCK 9
With **right** side facing and Orange, working in end of rows on Blocks 8 and 6 and Back Loops Only of bound off edge on Block 5, pick up 32 sts: 33 sts.

Rows 1-5: K1 tbl, knit across to last st, slip 1.

Bind off all sts in **knit**, leaving last st on needle.

Instructions continued on page 8.

BLOCK 10

Working in Back Loops Only at end of rows on Blocks 9 and 7 and along bound off edge on Block 6, pick up 36 sts: 37 sts.

Rows 1-5: K1 tbl, knit across to last st, slip 1.

Refer to Basic Crochet Stitches, page 28.

Bind off all sts in **knit**, place last st onto crochet hook, slip st across end of rows on Block 10, join with slip st to first bound off st on Block 7, finish off.

Color Blocks II Dishcloth

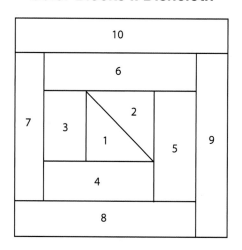

BRICK LATTICE DISHCLOTH

■■■□ INTERMEDIATE

Finished Size: 8¹/₂" (21.5 cm) square

MATERIALS

100% Cotton Medium Weight Yarn [4 MEDIUM]
[2 ounces, 98 yards
(56 grams, 89.5 meters) per ball]: 1 ball
Straight knitting needles, size 7 (4.5 mm) **or** size needed for gauge
Cable needle

GAUGE: In pattern,
18 sts = 4" (10 cm)

STITCH GUIDE
BACK CROSS (uses 4 sts)
Slip next 3 sts onto cable needle and hold at **back** of work, K1 from left needle, K3 from cable needle.
FRONT CROSS (uses 4 sts)
Slip next st onto cable needle and hold at **front** of work, K3 from left needle, K1 from cable needle.

DISHCLOTH
Cast on 44 sts.

Note: When instructed to slip a stitch, always slip as if to **purl** placing yarn in front or back as instructed.

Row 1 (Right side): Knit across to last st, WYF slip 1.

Row 2: K1 tbl *(Fig. 10, page 28)*, P2, YO *(Fig. 1b, page 26)*, (P6, YO) 6 times, P4, WYF slip 1: 51 sts.

Row 3: K1 tbl, K4, drop next st (YO), WYB slip 1, (K5, drop next st, WYB slip 1) across to last 2 sts, K1, WYF slip 1: 44 sts.

Row 4: K1 tbl, K1, WYF slip 1, (K5, WYF slip 1) across to last 5 sts, K4, WYF slip 1.

Row 5: K1 tbl, P4, WYB slip 1, (P5, WYB slip 1) across to last 2 sts, P1, WYF slip 1.

Row 6: K1 tbl, K1, WYF slip 1, (K5, WYF slip 1) across to last 5 sts, K4, WYF slip 1.

Row 7: K1 tbl, K1, work Back Cross, (K2, work Back Cross) across to last 2 sts, K1, WYF slip 1.

Row 8: K1 tbl, P8, YO, (P6, YO) 5 times, P4, WYF slip 1: 50 sts.

Row 9: K1 tbl, K4, drop next st, WYB slip 1, (K5, drop next st, WYB slip 1) across to last 8 sts, K7, WYF slip 1: 44 sts.

Row 10: K1 tbl, K7, WYF slip 1, (K5, WYF slip 1) across to last 5 sts, K4, WYF slip 1.

Row 11: K1 tbl, P4, WYB slip 1, (P5, WYB slip 1) across to last 8 sts, P7, WYF slip 1: 44 sts.

Row 12: K1 tbl, K7, WYF slip 1, (K5, WYF slip 1) across to last 5 sts, K4, WYF slip 1.

Row 13: K1 tbl, K4, work Front Cross, (K2, work Front Cross) across to last 5 sts, K4, WYF slip 1.

Rows 14-67: Repeat Rows 2-13, 4 times; then repeat Rows 2-7 once **more**.

Row 68: K1 tbl, purl across to last st, WYF slip 1.

Bind off all sts in **knit**.

REFLECTIONS DISHCLOTH

Note: When instructed to slip a stitch, always slip as if to **purl** with yarn forward.

◼◼◼◻ INTERMEDIATE

Finished Size: 8¹/₂" (21.5 cm) square

MATERIALS
100% Cotton Medium Weight Yarn
    [2 ounces, 98 yards
    (56 grams, 89.5 meters) per ball]: 1 ball
Straight knitting needles, size 8 (5 mm) **or** size
    needed for gauge
Cable needle

MEDIUM
4

GAUGE: In Garter Stitch,
        21 sts = 4" (10 cm)

STITCH GUIDE
RIGHT TWIST (uses 2 sts)
Slip next st onto cable needle and hold at **back** of work, K1 from left needle, P1 from cable needle.
LEFT TWIST (uses 2 sts)
Slip next st onto cable needle and hold at **front** of work, P1 from left needle, K1 from cable needle.

DISHCLOTH
Cast on 38 sts.

Rows 1-4: K1 tbl *(Fig. 10, page 28)*, knit across to last st, slip 1.

Row 5 (Right side)**:** K1 tbl, K2, P3, (K1, P3) 3 times, K2, P3, (K1, P3) 3 times, K2, slip 1.

Row 6: K1 tbl, K5, (P1, K3) 3 times, P2, (K3, P1) 3 times, K5, slip 1.

Row 7: K1 tbl, K2, (P2, work Right Twist) 4 times, (work Left Twist, P2) 4 times, K2, slip 1.

Row 8: K1 tbl, K4, P1, (K3, P1) 3 times, K2, P1, (K3, P1) 3 times, K4, slip 1.

Instructions continued on page 10.

Row 9: K1 tbl, K2, P1, (work Right Twist, P2) 4 times, work Left Twist, (P2, work Left Twist) 3 times, P1, K2, slip 1.

Row 10: K1 tbl, (K3, P1) 4 times, K4, P1, (K3, P1) 3 times, K3, slip 1.

Row 11: K1 tbl, K2, work Right Twist, (P2, work Right Twist) 3 times, P4, work Left Twist, (P2, work Left Twist) 3 times, K2, slip 1.

Row 12: K1 tbl, K2, P1, (K3, P1) 3 times, K6, P1, (K3, P1) 3 times, K2, slip 1.

Rows 13-16: K1 tbl, knit across to last st, slip 1.

Row 17: K1 tbl, K3, (P3, K1) 3 times, P6, (K1, P3) 3 times, K3, slip 1.

Row 18: K1 tbl, K2, P1, (K3, P1) 3 times, K6, P1, (K3, P1) 3 times, K2, slip 1.

Row 19: K1 tbl, K2, work Left Twist, (P2, work Left Twist) 3 times, P4, work Right Twist, (P2, work Right Twist) 3 times, K2, slip 1.

Row 20: K1 tbl, (K3, P1) 4 times, K4, P1, (K3, P1) 3 times, K3, slip 1.

Row 21: K1 tbl, K2, P1, (work Left Twist, P2) 4 times, work Right Twist, (P2, work Right Twist) 3 times, P1, K2, slip 1.

Row 22: K1 tbl, K4, P1, (K3, P1) 3 times, K2, P1, (K3, P1) 3 times, K4, slip 1.

Row 23: K1 tbl, K2, (P2, work Left Twist) 4 times, (work Right Twist, P2) 4 times, K2, slip 1.

Row 24: K1 tbl, K5, (P1, K3) 3 times, P2, (K3, P1) 3 times, K5, slip 1.

Rows 25-30: K1 tbl, knit across to last st, slip 1.

Rows 31-50: Repeat Rows 5-24.

Rows 51-55: K1 tbl, knit across to last st, slip 1.

Bind off all sts in **knit**.

SUNFLOWER POT HOLDER

⬤◼☐☐ **EASY**

Finished Size: 8¹/₂" (21.5 cm) square

MATERIALS

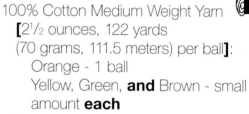

100% Cotton Medium Weight Yarn
[2¹/₂ ounces, 122 yards
(70 grams, 111.5 meters) per ball]:
Orange - 1 ball
Yellow, Green, **and** Brown - small amount **each**
[2 ounces, 98 yards
(56 grams, 89.5 meters) per ball]:
Variegated - 1 ball
Straight knitting needles, size 8 (5 mm) **or** size needed for gauge
Crochet hook, size H (5 mm)
Stitch holder
Yarn needle

GAUGE: In Garter Stitch,
18 sts = 4" (10 cm)

CHANGING COLORS
Work the last stitch to within one step of completion, hook new yarn *(Fig. A)* and draw through both loops on hook. Cut old yarn and work over both ends.

Fig. A

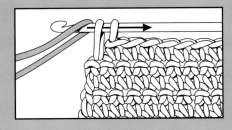

Note: When instructed to slip a stitch, always slip as if to **purl** with yarn forward.

FRONT
With Orange, cast on 39 sts.

Rows 1-5: K1 tbl *(Fig. 10, page 28)*, knit across to last st, slip 1.

Row 6: K1 tbl, K2, purl across to last 3 sts, K2, slip 1.

Row 7 (Right side)**:** K1 tbl, K5, P1, (K3, P1) across to last 4 sts, K3, slip 1.

Row 8: K1 tbl, K2, purl across to last 3 sts, K2, slip 1.

Row 9: K1 tbl, knit across to last st, slip 1.

Row 10: K1 tbl, K2, purl across to last 3 sts, K2, slip 1.

Row 11: K1 tbl, K3, P1, (K3, P1) across to last 6 sts, K5, slip 1.

Row 12: K1 tbl, K2, purl across to last 3 sts, K2, slip 1.

Row 13: K1 tbl, knit across to last st, slip 1.

Rows 14-53: Repeat Rows 6-13, 5 times.

Rows 54-56: K1 tbl, knit across to last st, slip 1.

Bind off all sts in **knit**.

FLOWER (Make 2)
Refer to Basic Crochet Stitches, page 28.

With crochet hook and Brown, ch 4; join with slip st to first ch to form a ring.

Rnd 1: Ch 1, 6 sc in ring, changing to Yellow in last sc made *(Fig. A)*; do **not** join, place marker to mark beginning of rnd *(See Markers, page 25)*.

Cut Brown.

Rnd 2: ★ Ch 5, sc in third ch from hook and in next 2 chs, slip st in Back Loop Only of next sc *(Fig. 15, page 28)*; repeat from ★ around; finish off leaving long end for sewing.

STEMS AND LEAVES
With Green, make a slip knot. With **right** side of Front facing, using photo as a guide for placement, and holding slip knot to **wrong** side, insert hook through pot holder, hook slip knot and pull through to Front. Slip st to form Stem and Leaf; finish off. Repeat for second Stem and Leaf.

Sew Flowers to top of Stems.

BACK
With Variegated, cast on 39 sts.

Rows 1-5: K1 tbl, knit across to last st, slip 1.

Row 6 (Right side)**:** K1 tbl, K2, purl across to last 3 sts, K2, slip 1.

Row 7: K1 tbl, knit across to last st, slip 1.

Rows 8-51: Repeat Rows 6 and 7, 22 times.

Rows 52-56: K1 tbl, knit across to last st, slip 1.

Bind off all sts in **knit**, slip last st onto crochet hook.

Joining Rnd: With **wrong** sides of Front and Back together, front facing, and working through both thicknesses, 2 sc in first corner, ★ sc evenly across to next corner, 2 sc in corner; repeat from ★ 2 times **more**, sc evenly across; join with slip st to first sc, finish off.

Blue Skies & Daisies
KITCHEN COLLECTION

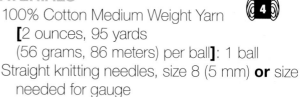

SASSY STRIPES DISHCLOTH

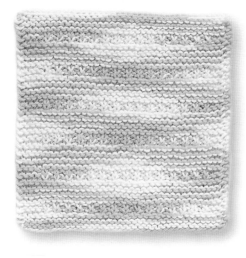

■■□□ **EASY**

Finished Size: 8¼" (21 cm) square

MATERIALS
100% Cotton Medium Weight Yarn **MEDIUM 4**
 [2 ounces, 95 yards
 (56 grams, 86 meters) per ball]: 1 ball
Straight knitting needles, size 8 (5 mm) **or** size
needed for gauge

GAUGE: In Garter Stitch,
 18 sts = 4" (10 cm)

DISHCLOTH
Cast on 38 sts.

Rows 1-6: Knit across.

Rows 7 and 8: K5, P1, (K1, P1) across to last 4 sts,
K4.

Rows 9-16: Knit across.

Rows 17-58: Repeat Rows 7-16, 4 times; then repeat
Rows 7 and 8 once **more**.

Rows 59-63: Knit across.

Bind off all sts in **knit**.

ZIG-ZAG DISHCLOTH

■■■□ **INTERMEDIATE**

Finished Size: 7½" (19 cm) square

MATERIALS
100% Cotton Medium Weight Yarn **MEDIUM 4**
 [2½ ounces, 120 yards
 (70 grams, 109 meters) per ball]: 1 ball
Straight knitting needles, size 8 (5 mm) **or** size
needed for gauge

GAUGE: In Garter Stitch,
 18 sts = 4" (10 cm)

STITCH GUIDE

LEFT TWIST (uses next 2 sts)
Working **behind** the first st on the left needle, knit into back of the second st *(Fig. A)* making sure **not** to let the sts drop off the left needle, then knit the first st *(Fig. B)* letting both sts drop off the needle.

Fig. A

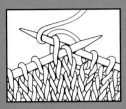

Fig. B

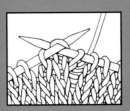

RIGHT TWIST (uses next 2 sts)
With yarn in **back** of work, separately slip 2 sts as if to **knit** *(Fig. 6a, page 27)*, then slip the 2 slipped sts back onto the left needle. Working in front of the first st on the left needle, knit the second st *(Fig. C)* making sure not to let the sts drop off the left needle, then knit the first st *(Fig. D)* letting both sts drop off the needle.

Fig. C

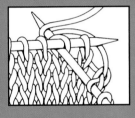

Fig. D

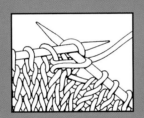

Note: When instructed to slip a stitch, always slip as if to **purl** with yarn forward.

DISHCLOTH

Cast on 38 sts.

Rows 1-4: K1 tbl *(Fig. 10, page 28)*, knit across to last st, slip 1.

Row 5: K1 tbl, K8, P 10, K6, P 10, K2, slip 1.

Row 6 (Right side)**:** K1 tbl, K2, ★ work Left Twist 5 times *(Figs. A & B)*, P6; repeat from ★ once **more**, K2, slip 1.

Row 7: K1 tbl, K8, P 10, K6, P 10, K2, slip 1.

Row 8: K1 tbl, K2, P1, work Left Twist 5 times, P6, work Left Twist 5 times, P5, K2, slip 1.

Row 9: K1 tbl, K7, P 10, K6, P 10, K3, slip 1.

Row 10: K1 tbl, K2, P2, work Left Twist 5 times, P6, work Left Twist 5 times, P4, K2, slip 1.

Row 11: K1 tbl, K6, P 10, K6, P 10, K4, slip 1.

Row 12: K1 tbl, K2, P3, work Left Twist 5 times, P6, work Left Twist 5 times, P3, K2, slip 1.

Row 13: K1 tbl, K5, P 10, K6, P 10, K5, slip 1.

Row 14: K1 tbl, K2, P4, work Left Twist 5 times, P6, work Left Twist 5 times, P2, K2, slip 1.

Row 15: K1 tbl, K4, P 10, K6, P 10, K6, slip 1.

Row 16: K1 tbl, K2, P5, work Left Twist 5 times, P6, work Left Twist 5 times, P1, K2, slip 1.

Row 17: K1 tbl, K3, P 10, K6, P 10, K7, slip 1.

Row 18: K1 tbl, K2, (P6, work Left Twist 5 times) twice, K2, slip 1.

Row 19: K1 tbl, K2, P 10, K6, P 10, K8, slip 1.

Row 20: K1 tbl, K2, ★ P6, work Right Twist 5 times *(Figs. C & D)*; repeat from ★ once **more**, K2, slip 1.

Row 21: K1 tbl, K2, P 10, K6, P 10, K8, slip 1.

Row 22: K1 tbl, K2, P5, work Right Twist 5 times, P6, work Right Twist 5 times, P1, K2, slip 1.

Row 23: K1 tbl, K3, P 10, K6, P 10, K7, slip 1.

Row 24: K1 tbl, K2, P4, work Right Twist 5 times, P6, work Right Twist 5 times, P2, K2, slip 1.

Row 25: K1 tbl, K4, P 10, K6, P 10, K6, slip 1.

Instructions continued on page 16.

Row 26: K1 tbl, K2, P3, work Right Twist 5 times, P6, work Right Twist 5 times, P3, K2, slip 1.

Row 27: K1 tbl, K5, P 10, K6, P 10, K5, slip 1.

Row 28: K1 tbl, K2, P2, work Right Twist 5 times, P6, work Right Twist 5 times, P4, K2, slip 1.

Row 29: K1 tbl, (K6, P 10) twice, K4, slip 1.

Row 30: K1 tbl, K2, P1, work Right Twist 5 times, P6, work Right Twist 5 times, P5, K2, slip 1.

Row 31: K1 tbl, K7, P 10, K6, P 10, K3, slip 1.

Row 32: K1 tbl, K2, (work Right Twist 5 times, P6) twice, K2, slip 1.

Row 33: K1 tbl, K8, P 10, K6, P 10, K2, slip 1.

Rows 34-47: Repeat Rows 6-19.

Row 48: K1 tbl, K2, P6, K 10, P6, K 12, slip 1.

Rows 49-51: K1 tbl, knit across to last st, slip 1.

Bind off all sts in **knit**.

AZTEC WEAVE DISHCLOTH

◖■◻◻ **EASY**

Finished Size: 8" (20.5 cm) square

MATERIALS
100% Cotton Medium Weight Yarn
   [2¹/₂ ounces, 122 yards
   (70 grams, 111.5 meters) per ball**]**: 1 ball
Straight knitting needles, size 7 (4.5 mm) **or** size
   needed for gauge

GAUGE: In pattern,
         18 sts = 4" (10 cm)

DISHCLOTH
Cast on 38 sts.

   Note: When instructed to slip a stitch, always slip as if to **purl** with yarn forward.

Rows 1-4: K1 tbl *(Fig. 10, page 28)*, knit across to last st, slip 1.

Rows 5-14: K1 tbl, K3, P1, (K1, P1) twice, ★ K7, P1, (K1, P1) twice; repeat from ★ once **more**, K4, slip 1.

Rows 15-24: K1 tbl, K9, P1, (K1, P1) twice, K7, P1, (K1, P1) twice, K 10, slip 1.

Rows 25-54: Repeat Rows 5-24 once, then repeat Rows 5-14 once **more**.

Rows 55-59: K1 tbl, knit across to last st, slip 1.

Bind off all sts in **knit**.

DESERT TWEED DISHCLOTH

Finished Size: 9¹/₂" (24 cm) square

MATERIALS

100% Cotton Medium Weight Yarn
[2¹/₂ ounces, 120 yards
(70 grams, 109 meters) per ball]: 1 ball
Color A (Blue)
[2 ounces, 95 yards
(56 grams, 86 meters) per ball]: 1 ball
Color B (Variegated)
12" (30.5 cm) Double-pointed knitting needles,
size 7 (4.5 mm) **or** size needed for gauge

MEDIUM 4

GAUGE: In pattern,
18 sts = 4" (10 cm)

DISHCLOTH

With Color A, cast on 43 sts; **turn**.

Note: Even numbered rows are worked using Color A, and odd numbered rows are worked using Color B. When both working yarns are on the **same** end of the needle after stitching across a row, you will need to **turn** the work to knit the next row. When working yarns are on **opposite** ends of the needle, you will need to **slide** the stitches to your right to knit the next row.

Row 1: With Color B, knit across; **slide**.

Row 2: With Color A, purl across; **turn**.

Row 3: With Color B, purl across; **slide**.

Row 4: With Color A, knit across; **turn**.

Row 5: With Color B, K4, P1, (K1, P1) across to last 4 sts, K4; **slide**.

Row 6 (Right side): With Color A, P3, K1, (P1, K1) across to last 3 sts, P3; **turn**.

Row 7: With Color B, P3, K1, (P1, K1) across to last 3 sts, P3; **slide**.

Row 8: With Color A, K4, P1, (K1, P1) across to last 4 sts, K4; **turn**.

Rows 9-60: Repeat Rows 5-8, 13 times.

Rows 61-64: Repeat Rows 1-4.

With Color A, bind off all sts in **knit**.

ELEGANT LINEN POT HOLDER

⬤⬤⬤◻ INTERMEDIATE

Finished Size: 8" (20.5 cm) square

MATERIALS
100% Cotton Medium Weight Yarn **MEDIUM 4**
[2 ounces, 95 yards
(56 grams, 86 meters) per ball]: 2 balls
Straight knitting needles, size 7 (4.5 mm) **or** size
needed for gauge

GAUGE: In pattern,
20 sts = 4" (10 cm)

POT HOLDER
Cast on 37 sts.

Note: When instructed to slip a stitch,
always slip as if to **purl** with yarn forward
unless otherwise instructed.

Rows 1-4: K1 tbl *(Fig. 10, page 28)*, knit across to
last st, slip 1.

Row 5 (Wrong side)**:** K1 tbl, K2, knit/purl increase
(Fig. 4, page 26) in each stitch across to last 3 sts,
K2, slip 1: 68 sts.

Rows 6 and 7: K1 tbl, K3, slip 1, (K1, slip 1) across
to last 3 sts, K2, slip 1.

Rows 8 and 9: K1 tbl, K3, (slip 3, K1) across to last
4 sts, slip 1, K2, slip 1.

Row 10: K1 tbl, K3, slip 1, K1, (slip 3, K1) across
to last 6 sts, slip 1, K1; **turn**, leave remaining 4 sts
unworked.

Row 11: Slip 1, K1, (slip 3, K1) across to last 6 sts,
slip 1, K1; **turn**, leave remaining 4 sts unworked.

Row 12: Slip 3, (K1, slip 3) across to last 5 sts, K1,
slip 1, K2, slip 1.

Row 13: K1 tbl, K3, slip 3, (K1, slip 3) across to last
5 sts, K1, slip 1, K2, slip 1.

Rows 14-25: Repeat Rows 10-13, 3 times.

Row 26: K1 tbl, K3, slip 1, (K1, slip 1) across to last
3 sts, K2, slip 1.

Row 27: K1 tbl, K3, ★ (slip 1, K1) 7 times, slip 1, work
Tacking St; repeat from ★ 2 times **more**, (slip 1, K1)
6 times, slip 1, K2, slip 1.

Rows 28-114: Repeat Rows 6-27, 3 times; then
repeat Rows 6-26 once **more**.

Row 115: Slip 1, K2, SSK *(Figs. 6a-c, page 27)*
across to last 3 sts, K2, slip 1: 37 sts.

Rows 116-119: K1 tbl, knit across to last st, slip 1.

Bind off all sts in **knit**.

Hot Chili Peppers
KITCHEN COLLECTION

HOT CHILI DISHCLOTH

■■■□ INTERMEDIATE

Finished Size: 9¹/₂" x 8¹/₂" (23 cm x 21.5 cm)

MATERIALS

100% Cotton Medium Weight Yarn
 [2 ounces, 95 yards
 (56 grams, 86 meters) per ball**]**:
 Variegated - 1 ball
 [2¹/₂ ounces 120 yards
 (70 grams, 109 meters) per ball**]**:
 Yellow - 1 ball
Straight knitting needles, size 7 (4.5 mm) **or** size
 needed for gauge
Crochet hook, size H (5 mm)

Note: When instructed to slip a stitch,
always slip as if to **purl** placing yarn in
front or back as instructed.

GAUGE: In pattern,
 18 sts = 4" (10 cm)

DISHCLOTH

With Varigated, cast on 42 sts.

Row 1 (Right side)**:** Knit across.

Row 2: P5, YO *(Fig. 1b, page 26)*, P7, (YO, P4,
YO, P7) twice, (YO, P4) twice: 49 sts.

Row 3: With Yellow, K4, drop next st (YO),
WYF slip 1, ★ K3, drop next st, WYF slip 1, K6,
drop next st, WYF slip 1; repeat from ★ 2 times
more, K4: 42 sts.

Row 4: K4, WYF slip 1, (K6, WYF slip 1, K3,
WYF slip 1) 3 times, K4.

Row 5: P4, WYB slip 1, (P3, WYB slip 1, P6,
WYB slip 1) 3 times, P4.

Row 6: Repeat Row 4.

Row 7: With Variegated, knit across.

Row 8: P3, YO, P4, (YO, P7, YO, P4) 3 times, YO,
P2: 50 sts.

Row 9: With Yellow, K2, drop next st, WYF slip 1,
K3, drop next st, WYF slip 1, ★ K6, drop next st,
WYF slip 1, K3, drop next st, WYF slip 1; repeat
from ★ 2 times **more**, K2: 42 sts.

Row 10: K2, WYF slip 1, K3, WYF slip 1, (K6,
WYF slip 1, K3, WYF slip 1) 3 times, K2.

Row 11: P2, WYB slip 1, P3, WYB slip 1, (P6,
WYB slip 1, P3, WYB slip 1) 3 times, P2.

Row 12: Repeat Row 10.

Row 13: With Variegated, knit across.

Instructions continued on page 20.

Row 14: P5, YO, P4, (YO, P7, YO, P4) across: 49 sts.

Row 15: With Yellow, K4, drop next st, WYF slip 1, ★ K6, drop next st, WYF slip 1, K3, drop next st, WYF slip 1; repeat from ★ 2 times **more**, K4: 42 sts.

Row 16: K4, WYF slip 1, (K3, WYF slip 1, K6, WYF slip 1) 3 times, K4.

Row 17: P4, WYB slip 1, (P6, WYB slip 1, P3, WYB slip 1) 3 times, P4.

Row 18: Repeat Row 16.

Row 19: With Variegated, knit across.

Row 20: P7, YO, (P4, YO, P7, YO) 3 times, P2: 49 sts.

Row 21: With Yellow, K2, drop next st, WYF slip 1, ★ K6, drop next st, WYF slip 1, K3, drop next st, WYF slip 1; repeat from ★ 2 times **more**, K6: 42 sts.

Row 22: K6, WYF slip 1, (K3, WYF slip 1, K6, WYF slip 1) 3 times, K2.

Row 23: P2, WYB slip 1, P6, (WYB slip 1, P3, WYB slip 1, P6) 3 times.

Row 24: Repeat Row 22.

Row 25: With Variegated, knit across.

Row 26: P9, (YO, P4, YO, P7) 3 times 48 sts.

Row 27: With Yellow, K7, drop next st, WYF slip 1, K3, drop next st, WYF slip 1, ★ K6, drop next st, WYF slip 1, K3, drop next st, WYF slip 1; repeat from ★ once **more**, K8: 42 sts.

Row 28: K8, WYF slip 1, K3, WYF slip 1, (K6, WYF slip 1, K3, WYF slip 1) twice, K7.

Row 29: P7, WYB slip 1, P3, WYB slip 1, (P6, WYB slip 1, P3, WYB slip 1) twice, P8.

Row 30: Repeat Row 28.

Row 31: With Variegated, knit across.

Row 32: P4, YO, (P7, YO, P4, YO) 3 times, P5: 49 sts.

Row 33: With Yellow, K5, drop next st, WYF slip 1, ★ K3, drop next st, WYF slip 1, K6, drop next st, WYF slip 1; repeat from ★ 2 times **more**, K3: 42 sts.

Row 34: K3, WYF slip 1, (K6, WYF slip 1, K3, WYF slip 1) 3 times, K5.

Row 35: P5, WYB slip 1, P3, (WYB slip 1, P6, WYB slip 1, P3) 3 times.

Row 36: Repeat Row 34.

Row 37: With Variegated, knit across.

Row 38: P6, YO, (P7, YO, P4, YO) 3 times, P3: 49 sts.

Row 39: With Yellow, (K3, drop next st, WYF slip 1) twice, K6, drop next st, WYF slip 1, ★ K3, drop next st, WYF slip 1, K6, drop next st, WYF slip 1; repeat from ★ once **more**, K5: 42 sts.

Row 40: K5, WYF slip 1, (K6, WYF slip 1, K3, WYF slip 1) 3 times, K3.

Row 41: (P3, WYB slip 1) twice, P6, WYB slip 1, (P3, WYB slip 1, P6, WYB slip 1) twice, P5.

Row 42: Repeat Row 40.

Row 43: With Variegated, knit across.

Row 44: (P4, YO) twice, P7, YO, (P4, YO, P7, YO) twice, P5: 49.

Row 45: With Yellow, K5, drop next st, WYF slip 1, ★ K6, drop next st, WYF slip 1, K3, drop next st, WYF slip 1; repeat from ★ 2 times **more**, K3: 42 sts.

Row 46: K3, WYF slip 1, (K3, WYF slip 1, K6, WYF slip 1) 3 times, K5.

Row 47: P5, WYB slip 1, (P6, WYB slip 1, P3, WYB slip 1) 3 times, P3.

Row 48: Repeat Row 46.

Row 49: With Variegated, knit across.

Row 50: P6, YO, (P4, YO, P7, YO) 3 times, P3: 49 sts.

Row 51: With Yellow, K3, drop next st, WYF slip 1, ★ K6, drop next st, WYF slip 1, K3, drop next st, WYF slip 1; repeat from ★ 2 times **more**, K5: 42 sts.

Row 52: K5, WYF slip 1, K3, (WYF slip 1, K6, WYF slip 1, K3) 3 times.

Row 53: P3, WYB slip 1, (P6, WYB slip 1, P3, WYB slip 1) 3 times, P5.

Row 54: Repeat Row 52.

Row 55: With Variegated, knit across.

Row 56: P8, YO, P4, YO, (P7, YO, P4, YO) twice, P8: 48 sts.

Row 57: With Yellow, K8, drop next st, WYF slip 1, K3, drop next st, WYF slip 1, ★ K6, drop next st, WYF slip 1, K3, drop next st, WYF slip 1; repeat from ★ once **more**, K7: 42 sts.

Row 58: K7, WYF slip 1, K3, WYF slip 1, (K6, WYF slip 1, K3, WYF slip 1) twice, K8.

Row 59: P8, WYB slip 1, P3, WYB slip 1, (P6, WYB slip 1, P3, WYB slip 1) twice, P7.

Row 60: Repeat Row 58.

Row 61: With Variegated, knit across.

Row 62: P3, YO, (P7, YO, P4, YO) 3 times, P6: 49 sts.

Row 63: With Yellow, K6, drop next st, WYF slip 1, ★ K3, drop next st, WYF slip 1, K6, drop next st, WYF slip 1; repeat from ★ 2 times **more**, K2: 42 sts.

Row 64: K2, WYF slip 1, K6, (WYF slip 1, K3, WYF slip 1, K6) 3 times.

Row 65: P6, WYB slip 1, (P3, WYB slip 1, P6, WYB slip 1) 3 times, P2.

Row 66: K2, WYF slip 1, K6, (WYF slip 1, K3, WYF slip 1, K6) 3 times, cut Yellow.

Row 67: With Variegated, knit across.

Row 68: Purl across.

Bind off all sts in **knit**, place last st onto crochet hook.

Refer to Basic Crochet Stitches, page 28.

EDGING: With Variegated, sc evenly around working 2 sc in each corner; join with slip st to first sc, finish off.

HOT CHILI POT HOLDER

●●●◻ **INTERMEDIATE**

Finished Size: 8¹/₂" (21.5 cm) square

MATERIALS

100% Cotton Medium Weight Yarn
[2¹/₂ ounces, 122 yards
(70 grams, 109 meters) per ball]:
Yellow - 1 ball
Red **and** Green - small amount **each**
[2 ounces, 98 yards
(56 grams, 86 meters) per ball]:
Variegated - 1 ball
Straight knitting needles, size 7 (4.5 mm) **or** size
needed for gauge
Crochet hook, size H (5 mm)
Stitch holder
Yarn needle

GAUGE: In Garter Stitch,
18 sts = 4" (10 cm)

FRONT
With Yellow, cast on 39 sts.

Rows 1-5: Knit across.

Row 6: K2, purl across to last 3 sts, K3.

Row 7 (Right side)**:** K4, P1, (K3, P1) across to
last 6 sts, K6.

Row 8: K3, purl across to last 3 sts, K3.

Row 9: Knit across.

Row 10: K3, purl across to last 3 sts, K3.

Row 11: K6, P1, (K3, P1) across to last 4 sts, K4.

Row 12: K3, purl across to last 3 sts, K3.

Row 13: Knit across.

Rows 14-53: Repeat Rows 6-13, 5 times.

Rows 54-56: Knit across.

Bind off all sts in **knit**.

CHILI PEPPER (Make 1 Red and 1 Green)
Cast on 2 sts.

Rows 1 and 2: Knit across.

Row 3 (Right side)**:** K1, knit increase *(Figs. 2a & b, page 26)*: 3 sts.

Rows 4-10: Knit across.

Row 11: K1, knit increase, K1: 4 sts.

Rows 12-20: Knit across.

Row 21: K2, knit increase, K1: 5 sts.

Rows 22-27: Knit across.

Bind off all sts in **knit**, place last st onto crochet hook.

Refer to Basic Crochet Stitches, page 28.

With **right** side facing, slip st across to center of last row, ch 4; finish off leaving a long end for sewing.

BACK
With Variegated, cast on 39 sts.

Rows 1-58: Knit across.

Bind off all sts in **knit**, slip last st onto st holder.

FINISHING

With **right** side facing and using photo as a guide for placement, sew Chili Peppers to Front using long end.

Joining Rnd: Place loop from st holder onto crochet hook. With **wrong** sides of Front and Back together, Front facing, matching cast on edges, and working through **both** thicknesses, 2 sc in first corner, ★ sc evenly across to next corner, 2 sc in corner; repeat from ★ 2 times **more**, sc evenly across, join with slip st to first sc, ch 10, slip st in next sc; finish off.

HOT CHILI HAND TOWEL

■■■□ INTERMEDIATE

Finished Size: 11¹/₂" wide x 15" high when buttoned
        (29 cm x 38 cm)

MATERIALS

100% Cotton Medium Weight Yarn
[2¹/₂ ounces, 122 yards
(70 grams, 109 meters) per ball]:
    Yellow - 1 ball
    Red **and** Green - small amount **each**
[2 ounces, 98 yards
(56 grams, 86 meters) per ball]:
    Variegated - 1 ball
Straight knitting needles, size 7 (4.5 mm) **or** size
    needed for gauge
Crochet hook, size H (5 mm)
⁵/₈" (16 mm) Button

GAUGE: In pattern,
        18 sts = 4" (10 cm)

Note: When instructed to slip a stitch, always slip as if to **purl** placing yarn in front or back as instructed.

HAND TOWEL

With Variegated, cast on 57 sts.

Row 1: Purl across.

Row 2 (Right side)**:** With Yellow, K4, WYB slip 1, (K5, WYB slip 1) across to last 4 sts, K4.

Row 3: K4, WYF slip 1, (K5, WYF slip 1) across to last 4 sts, K4.

Row 4: P4, WYB slip 1, (P5, WYB slip 1) across to last 4 sts, P4.

Row 5: Repeat Row 3.

Row 6: With Variegated, knit across.

Row 7: Purl across.

Row 8: With Yellow, K1, WYB slip 1, (K5, WYB slip 1) across to last st, K1.

Row 9: K1, WYF slip 1, (K5, WYF slip 1) across to last st, K1.

Row 10: P1, WYB slip 1, (P5, WYB slip 1) across to last st, P1.

Row 11: Repeat Row 9.

Row 12: With Variegated, knit across.

Instructions continued on page 24.

Rows 13-103: Repeat Rows 1-12, 7 times; then repeat Rows 1-7 once **more**, cut Yellow.

Row 104: P2 tog (*Fig. 7, page 27*), purl across: 56 sts.

Row 105: SSK 14 times (*Figs. 6a-c, page 27*), K2 tog 14 times (*Fig. 5, page 26*): 28 sts.

Rows 106-108: Knit across.

Row 109: SSK 7 times, K2 tog 7 times: 14 sts.

Row 110: Knit across.

Place marker around any st to mark Row 110 for placement of Chili Peppers.

Rows 111-134: Knit across.

Row 135: K7, YO (*Fig. 1a, page 26*), K7: 15 sts.

Row 136: Knit across.

Rows 137-141: K2 tog, knit across to last 2 sts, SSK: 5 sts.

Bind off all sts in **knit**, place last st onto crochet hook.

Refer to Basic Crochet Stitches, page 28.

Trim: Sc evenly around; join with slip st to first sc, finish off.

FIRST CHILI PEPPER
Stem
With **right** side facing, Variegated, and last row toward you, pick up 3 sts near center of marked row. Slip sts onto left needle.

Keep **right** side facing you, do **not** turn.

Row 1: Knit across, slip sts just made back onto left needle.

Repeat Row 1 until Stem measures ¹/₂" (1.5 cm).

Cut Variegated.

Pepper
Row 1: With Red, knit increase twice (*Figs. 2a & b, page 26*), K1, slip sts back onto left needle: 5 sts.

Row 2: P5, slip sts back onto left needle.

Row 3: Purl increase (*Fig. 3, page 26*), P2, purl increase, P1, slip sts back onto left needle: 7 sts.

Row 4: P7, slip sts back onto left needle.

Row 5: K7, slip sts back onto left needle.

Row 6: K2 tog, K3, SSK, slip sts back onto left needle: 5 sts.

Rows 7 and 8: K5, slip sts back onto left needle.

Row 9: K2 tog, K1, SSK, slip sts back onto left needle: 3 sts.

Row 10: K3, slip sts back onto left needle.

Row 11: K3.

Pass second and third sts over first st. Cut yarn, pulling yarn end through loop to secure.

SECOND CHILI PEPPER
Stem
With **right** side facing, Variegated, and last row toward you, pick up 3 sts near center of marked row. Slip sts onto left needle.

Keep **right** side facing you, do **not** turn.

Row 1: Knit across, slip sts just made back onto left needle.

Repeat Row 1 until Stem measures 2" (5 cm).

Cut Variegated.

Pepper
Row 1: With Green, knit increase twice, K1, slip sts back onto left needle: 5 sts.

Complete same as First Chili Pepper.

FINISHING
Using photo as a guide, sew button above Chili Peppers.

General Instructions

ABBREVIATIONS

ch(s)	chain(s)
cm	centimeters
K	knit
P	purl
sc	single crochet(s)
SSK	slip, slip, knit
st(s)	stitch(es)
tbl	thrugh the back loop
tog	together
WYB	with yarn in back
WYF	with yarn in front
YO	yarn over

★ — work instructions following ★ as many **more** times as indicated in addition to the first time.

( ) or **[ ]** — work enclosed instructions **as many** times as specified by the number immediately following **or** work all enclosed instructions in the stitch or space indicated **or** contains explanatory remarks.

colon (:) — the number(s) given after a colon at the end of a row or round denote(s) the number of stitches you should have on that row or round.

GAUGE

The preceding instructions are written for 100% cotton medium weight yarn. The gauge and finished size are given for your convenience and are meant only as a guide. Gauge is not of great importance for these projects; your dishcloths, potholders, or dishtowels may be a little larger or smaller without changing the overall effect.

MARKERS

Markers are used to help distinguish the beginning of each round being worked. Place a 2" (5 cm) scrap piece of yarn before the first stitch of each round, moving marker after each round is complete.

CROCHET TERMINOLOGY	
UNITED STATES	**INTERNATIONAL**
single crochet =	double crochet
slip stitch =	single crochet

Yarn Weight Symbol & Names	SUPER FINE 1	FINE 2	LIGHT 3	MEDIUM 4	BULKY 5	SUPER BULKY 6
Type of Yarns in Category	Sock, Fingering Baby	Sport, Baby	DK, Light Worsted	Worsted, Afghan, Aran	Chunky, Craft, Rug	Bulky, Roving

KNIT TERMINOLOGY	
UNITED STATES	**INTERNATIONAL**
gauge =	tension
bind off =	cast off
yarn over (YO) =	yarn forward (yfwd) **or** yarn around needle (yrn)

KNITTING NEEDLES																
U.S.	0	1	2	3	4	5	6	7	8	9	10	10½	11	13	15	17
U.K.	13	12	11	10	9	8	7	6	5	4	3	2	1	00	000	---
Metric - mm	2	2.25	2.75	3.25	3.5	3.75	4	4.5	5	5.5	6	6.5	8	9	10	12.75

■□□□ **BEGINNER**	Projects for first-time knitters using basic knit and purl stitches. Minimal shaping.
■■□□ **EASY**	Projects using basic stitches, repetitive stitch patterns, simple color changes, and simple shaping and finishing.
■■■□ **INTERMEDIATE**	Projects with a variety of stitches, such as basic cables and lace, simple intarsia, double-pointed needles and knitting in the round needle techniques, mid-level shaping and finishing.
■■■■ **EXPERIENCED**	Projects using advanced techniques and stitches, such as short rows, fair isle, more intricate intarsia, cables, lace patterns, and numerous color changes.

YARN OVERS

After a knit stitch, before a knit stitch

Bring the yarn forward **between** the needles, then back **over** the top of the right hand needle, so that it is now in position to knit the next stitch **(Fig. 1a)**.

Fig. 1a

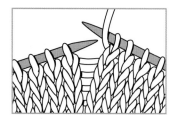

After a purl stitch, before a purl stitch

Take yarn **over** the right hand needle to the back, then forward **under** it, so that it is now in position to purl the next stitch **(Fig. 1b)**.

Fig. 1b

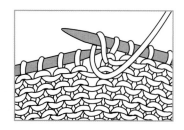

INCREASES

The increases in this book use one stitch to make two stitches. You will have two stitches on the right needle for the one stitch worked off the left needle. The type of increase used depends on the stitch needed to maintain the pattern.

KNIT INCREASE

Knit the next stitch but do **not** slip the old stitch off the left needle **(Fig. 2a)**. Insert the right needle into the back loop of the same stitch and knit it **(Fig. 2b)**, then slip the old stitch off the left needle.

Fig. 2a

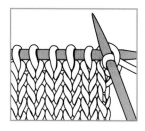

Fig. 2b

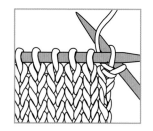

PURL INCREASE

Purl the next stitch but do **not** slip the old stitch off the left needle. Insert the right needle into the back loop of the same stitch and purl it **(Fig. 3)**, then slip the old stitch off the left needle.

Fig. 3

KNIT/PURL INCREASE

Knit the next stitch but do **not** slip the old stitch off the left needle. With yarn forward, insert the right needle into the **front** loop of the **same** stitch from **back** to **front** **(Fig. 4)** and purl it. Slip the old stitch off the left needle.

Fig. 4

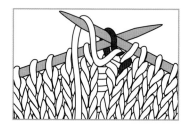

DECREASES
KNIT 2 TOGETHER

  (abbreviated K2 tog)

Insert the right needle into the **front** of the first two stitches on the left needle as if to **knit** **(Fig. 5)**, then **knit** them together as if they were one stitch.

Fig. 5

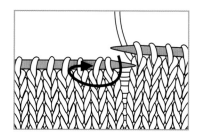

SLIP, SLIP, KNIT
(abbreviated SSK)
(With yarn in back of work,) separately slip two stitches as if to **knit** *(Fig. 6a)*. Insert the left needle into the **front** of both slipped stitches *(Fig. 6b)* and knit them together as if they were one stitch *(Fig. 6c)*.

Fig. 6a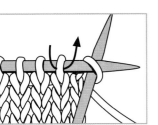

Fig. 6b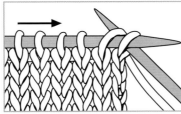

Fig. 6c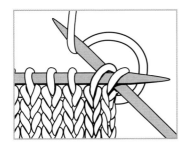

PURL 2 TOGETHER
(abbreviated P2 tog)
Insert the right needle into the front of the first two stitches on the left needle as if to **purl** *(Fig. 7)*, then purl them together as if they were one stitch.

Fig. 7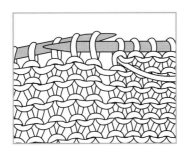

PICKING UP STITCHES
When instructed to pick up stitches, insert the needle from the **front** to the **back** under two strands at the edge of the worked piece *(Figs. 8a & b)*. Put the yarn around the needle as if to **knit**, then bring the needle with the yarn back through the stitch to the right side, resulting in a stitch on the needle.
Repeat this along the edge, picking up the required number of stitches.
A crochet hook may be helpful to pull yarn through.

Fig. 8a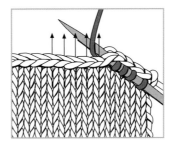

Fig. 8b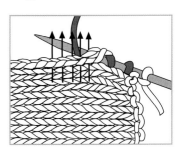

PICKING UP STITCHES THROUGH THE BACK LOOPS ONLY
When instructed to pick up stitches through the back loops only, insert the needle from the **front** to the **back** under the back loop at the edge of the worked piece *(Figs. 9a & b)*. Put the yarn around the needle as if to **knit**, then bring the needle with the yarn back through the stitch to the right side, resulting in a stitch on the needle.
Repeat this along the edge, picking up the required number of stitches.
A crochet hook may be helpful to pull yarn through.

Fig. 9a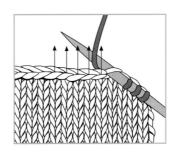

Fig. 9b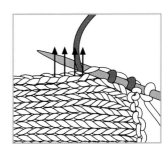

KNITTING THROUGH BACK LOOP ONLY

(abbreviated tbl)

With yarn in back, insert the right needle into the **back** of the next st from **front** to **back** *(Fig. 10)* and knit it.

Fig. 10

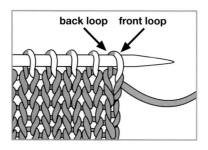

BASIC CROCHET STITCHES

CHAIN

To work a chain stitch, begin with a slip knot on the hook. Bring the yarn **over** hook from back to front, catching the yarn with the hook and turning the hook slightly toward you to keep the yarn from slipping off. Draw the yarn through the slip knot *(Fig. 11)* (first **chain st made, *abbreviated ch*)**.

Fig. 11

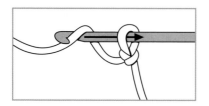

SLIP STITCH

To work a slip stitch, insert hook in stitch indicated, YO and draw through st and through loop on hook *(Fig. 12)* (slip stitch made, *abbreviated slip st*).

Fig. 12

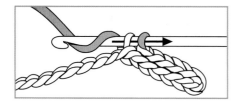

SINGLE CROCHET

Insert hook in stitch indicated, YO and pull up a loop, YO and draw through both loops on hook *(Fig. 13)* (single crochet made, *abbreviated sc*).

Fig. 13

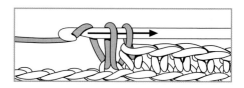

FINISH OFF

When you complete your last stitch, cut the yarn leaving a long end. Bring the loose end through the last loop on your hook and tighten it *(Fig. 14)*.

Fig. 14

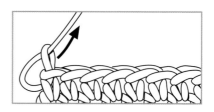

BACK LOOP ONLY

Work only in loop(s) indicated by arrow **(Fig. 15)**.

Fig. 15

Production Team: Instructional Writer - Jean Lewis; Technical Editor - Lois J. Long; Senior Graphic Artist - Chaska Richardson Lucas; Graphic Artists - Stephanie Johnson and Amy Gerke; Photo Stylist - Cassie Francioni; and Photographer - Jason Masters

Items made and instructions tested by Katie Galucki and Sue Galucki.

We have made every effort to ensure that these instructions are accurate and complete. We cannot, however, be responsible for human error, typographical mistakes, or variations in individual work.

ISBN13: 978-1-60140-482-4   ISBN10: 1-60140-482-4